I'm Nobody!
Who Are You?

I'm Nobody! Who Are You?

Poems of Emily Dickinson for Children

Illustrated by Rex Schneider

With an Introduction by Richard B. Sewall
Professor of English, Emeritus, Yale University

DISCARD

Stemmer House PUBLISHERS, INC.

Owings Mills, Maryland 1978

Copyright © 1978 by Stemmer House Publishers, Inc.

Illustrations copyright © 1978 by Rex Schneider

"Make me a picture of the sun," "I robbed the woods," "The mountain sat upon the plain," "The judge is like the owl" and "Two butterflies went out at noon" reprinted by permission of the publishers and the Trustees of Amherst College from *The Poems of Emily Dickinson,* edited by Thomas H. Johnson, Cambridge, Mass.: The Belknap Press of Harvard University Press, Copyright © 1951, 1955 by the President and Fellows of Harvard College.
"Funny to be a century" and "Too much of proof affronts belief" copyright 1929, © 1957 by Mary L. Hampson. From *Poems* by Emily Dickinson, Revised Edition, edited by Martha Dickinson, by permission of Little, Brown and Co.

Inquiries should be directed to
Stemmer House Publishers, Inc.
2627 Caves Road
Owings Mills, Maryland 21117

A Barbara Holdridge book

Printed and bound in the United States of America
First Printing, 1978
Second Printing, 1979
Third Printing, 1981

Published simultaneously in Canada by George J. McLeod, Limited, Don Mills, Ontario

Library of Congress Cataloging in Publication Data

Dickinson, Emily, 1830-1886.
    I'm nobody! Who are you?

    "A Barbara Holdridge book."
    SUMMARY: An illustrated collection of poems by an outstanding nineteenth-century American poet whose works were published posthumously.
    [1. American poetry]   I. Schneider, Rex.
II. Title.
PS1541.I54 1978   811'.4   78-6828
ISBN 0-916144-21-6
ISBN 0-916144-22-4 pbk.

Contents

Introduction

When Emily Dickinson wrote "I'm nobody," she was fooling just a little bit, but in another way she was quite serious.

She was a grown woman when she wrote it and knew very well that she was "somebody" in the town of Amherst, Massachusetts, where she was born in 1830 and died in 1886. Her grandfather had helped found Amherst College. Her father was its treasurer and one of the leading lawyers of the town, and for a while was a Congressman in Washington. Emily had a brilliant brother, Austin, three years older than she, who became a lawyer like his father. Her sister Lavinia, whom everybody called Vinnie, was known as the pepper-pot of the town because of her wit and sharp tongue. Emily's mother won prizes for her cooking. The family lived in one of the finest houses in town and was admired and looked up to by everyone. She was "somebody," all right.

And then too, Emily was the brightest girl in Amherst Academy, the school she attended before Mount Holyoke College. She loved her studies, especially botany, and kept a fine herbarium—pressed flowers, leaves and grasses. In the spring the woods around Amherst are full of wildflowers, like the ones Emily wrote about in the poem on page 7: "Pink, small, and punctual" (it's arbutus!). In the poem on page 65, "I robbed the woods," she tells how she'd "rob" them for things to write poems about. All in all, she loved her home, she loved Amherst, and she hated to leave it. She almost never did.

When she was still a girl, maybe fifteen or sixteen, she began to write poems. Nobody in her family encouraged her. They weren't interested in writing much of anything but letters and legal papers, and her mother, who spent most of her time keeping house, didn't even like to write letters! No one, apparently, took Emily's interest seriously—except one young man, nine years older than she, named Benjamin Franklin Newton. He was a law student in her father's office and saw a good deal of her about the time she started writing. But he left Amherst when she was eighteen, and he died four years later, much to Emily's sorrow. Shortly before he died, he must have written her a letter. "My dying Tutor told me that he would like to live till I had been a poet," she once said. He seemed to know that some day she would be famous. He wrote in her autograph album, "All can write Autographs, but few (can write) paragraphs; for we are mostly *names.*"

She's famous now, but it was hard then. Grown women were only supposed to keep house and do the cooking, like Emily's mother. Still, as Emily grew older, she found herself writing more and more. It meant everything to her. At one time she was writing almost a poem a day. She sent a few to some literary men, but no one was interested enough to get them published. So she put them in her bureau drawer and decided not to bother anybody else about them.

For this reason, Emily was serious when she wrote "I'm nobody! Who are you?" She really made up her mind to be a "nobody." Let others be big frogs if they wanted to. She would be herself, send a poem now and then in a letter to a friend, and not try to publish any. It wasn't until 1955, almost seventy years after her death, that all of her poems were finally published.

So she wrote and wrote, and tended her garden, and did housework, and made bread for her father. Often she'd be the last one to bed, writing poems or letters to the tune (as she once wrote) of the snores of father and mother and Vinnie and Austin!

After she died, Vinnie found almost two thousand poems in her bureau drawer, most of them complete, but with no titles since she didn't feel the need for any.

The poems themselves aren't as easy as "Jack and Jill" or "Mary Had a Little Lamb." You'll want to read some of them again and again to understand them better.

Something happens in every one of them, and the interesting thing is to find out *what.* Sometimes a poem will tell a story, like the one on page 27, "You've seen balloons set, haven't you?" Balloons were very exciting. In Emily's time, long before airplanes were invented, people would come for miles to see a balloon go up, as Emily may have done when they set one loose in Northampton, eight miles from Amherst. In the poem she tells how the balloon rose in the air, the crowd below staring and applauding. When the balloon hit a tree and plunged into the "sea," nobody was hurt—"'Twas only a balloon." Everybody shrugged and went back to work, not caring anything for the gay and beautiful thing that was lost. But for the poet the sight was at the same time sad and thrilling—and beautiful. (So is the poem!)

There is a poem on pages 36 to 38 that begins, "I started early, took my dog" (Emily had a big dog named Carlo). At the seashore, she imagines that mermaids greet her and ships hold out their "hempen hands" (really ropes) to her. But then the tide comes in (Old Man Neptune with his trident, as you see in the picture) and she is frightened and runs for home. She imagines that the sea follows her. But soon she is safe and sound, for the sea "withdrew," and her fright is over. Maybe the sea meant her no harm after all. It doesn't matter that (as she says in another poem) she never saw the sea; she is simply telling about how you have a fright and get over it.

Then there's the poem about the railroad (page 5), "I like to see it lap the miles." Railroads were new then, and the line had just reached Amherst. There was a big celebration, and Emily's father led the procession. Everybody was thrilled, including Emily. In the poem, she follows this new "iron horse" on its route as it goes through valleys and "cuts," and around mountains, and stops at water tanks (they were all steam engines in those days) to take on water, and blows its whistle at road crossings, and then stops, right on time, at the Amherst station! (Before then, only horses pulled loads, so it's quite natural to call the station a "stable.")

Another fine story-poem is the one about the thieves robbing the lonely house, "I know some lonely houses off the road," pages 49-51. "A narrow fellow in the grass," pages 53 and 54, is a snake story—how the poet feels when she meets a snake in the meadow. She can't understand why she likes all the animals ("nature's people") except snakes. They give her the shivers—"zero at the bone." I know children who love snakes and keep them as pets. But Emily didn't!

In the poem on pages 20-22, "A bird came down the walk," notice how carefully Emily watches him eating a worm, taking a drink of dew, avoiding a beetle, and then flying away the instant she moves to offer him a crumb. That's all that "happens"—but how interesting she makes it! She had a sharp eye.

So many of her poems are about things in nature. She sees them clearly, and she has new things to say about them all. The sunrise, a full moon, butterflies, a mountain, a blue jay, autumn, the frost, the sea, an owl—you can find poems in this book that tell about these things. In these poems, "what happens" is not a story, but it's a "happening" just the same. It "happens" in your mind and imagination. For instance, did you ever think that a mountain sitting on a plain was like a grandfather with children playing around his knee? Did you ever think of a blue jay as a military officer all dressed up in his fancy uniform? Or of butterflies as ships sailing to distant, unknown ports? Or of the beach as a rope that keeps the sea from going too far onto the land? Once you see these things the way Emily saw them, they begin to mean a lot more to you, and you enjoy them more.

Then there are poems that give you new thoughts about things, like books and words; or new ideas about feelings and emotions and states of mind—like hope ("the thing with feathers," page 78), and presentiment on page 43 (she makes that hard word easier to understand), and revery (page 29), and why people go to shows (page 57), and why it's just as well a century can't talk (page 59)!

Sometimes her mood is a sad one. In the poem "The bee is not afraid of me" (page 55), she asks why she finds herself weeping in the midst of all the lovely things of nature. (Sometimes people cry out of pure joy. Or perhaps they have a secret sorrow.) Sometimes she feels lonely and longs for someone to hold her close, as in the poems "My river runs to thee" (page 33) and "I hide myself within my flower" (page 41). Sometimes she feels quite lost, as in the poem about the little boat (page 40), which is really herself. Sometimes she cries for help (page 45): "Won't there *ever* be a morning? Am I to be sad like this *forever?* Won't somebody *tell* me?" But then, in another poem, the morning finally comes "and peace was paradise" (page 16). As in the poem about the rising tide, she gets over her fear and is herself again. Maybe just writing those poems helped.

As a matter of fact, she said in one of her letters that it *did.* That was one of the reasons that she wrote them. She gives another reason in the poem that begins "If I can stop one heart from breaking" (page 17). She knew what it was to be frightened and sad and lonely, and she felt that perhaps her poems could help other people who had those same troubles. She felt that people ought to share more, and love the world they lived in more. So, especially in the poems about nature, she tries to get people to look more carefully at the wonderful things around them, and hear the beautiful sounds, and sample the wonderful tastes. (The bee in "The pedigree of honey" (page 29), doesn't ask questions about the honey, he just *eats* it!) If only people would *live* life, she seems to be saying, they'd be a lot happier. So, in the poem "Make me a picture of the sun" (page 73) she's really talking to herself. She's saying, "Write a poem about the sun that will make chilly people feel warm! Write a poem about a robin that will make shut-in people hear him sing! My poems can do this for people!"

This is why she uses the words "prancing poetry" in the poem "There is no frigate like a book" (page 6). It "prances"—and it will make you prance! Poetry doesn't cost anything; even the poorest people can affort it. It's there for everybody to read and enjoy and be happy about—or, as she would say, "prance" to! As I hope you do with this book.

Bethany, Connecticut   Richard B. Sewall
March 1978

I'm Nobody!
Who Are You?

I'm nobody! Who are you?
Are you nobody, too?
Then there's a pair of us—don't tell!
They'd banish us, you know.

How dreary to be somebody!
How public, like a frog,
To tell your name the livelong day
To an admiring bog!

I like to see it lap the miles,
And lick the valleys up,
And stop to feed itself at tanks,
And then, prodigious, step

Around a pile of mountains,
And, supercilious, peer
In shanties by the sides of roads,
And then a quarry pare

To fit its sides, and crawl between,
Complaining all the while
In horrid, hooting stanza,
Then chase itself down hill

And neigh like Boanerges—
Then, punctual as a star,
Stop—docile and omnipotent—
At its own stable door.

There is no frigate like a book
To take us lands away,
Nor any coursers like a page
Of prancing poetry.
This traverse may the poorest take
Without oppress of toll—
How frugal is the chariot
That bears a human soul!

Pink, small, and punctual,
Aromatic, low,
Covert in April,
Candid in May,

Dear to the moss,
Known by the knoll,
Next to the robin
In every human soul.

Bold little beauty,
Bedecked with thee,
Nature forswears
Antiquity.

Too much of proof affronts belief.
The turtle will not try
Unless you leave him;
Then return—

And he has hauled away.

She sweeps with many-colored brooms,
And leaves the shreds behind.
Oh housewife in the evening West,
Come back, and dust the pond!

You dropped a purple ravelling in—
You dropped an amber thread—
And now you've littered all the East
With duds of emerald!

And still she plies her spotted brooms,
And still the aprons fly,
Till brooms fade softly into stars,
And then I come away.

The mountain sat upon the plain
In his tremendous chair,
His observation omnifold,
His inquest, everywhere.

The seasons played around his knees
Like children round a sire—
Grandfather of the days is he,
Of dawn the ancestor.

A prompt, executive bird is the jay,
Bold as a bailiff's hymn—
Brittle and brief in quality—
Warrant in every line.
Sitting a bough like a brigadier
Confident and straight—
Much is the mien of him in March
As a magistrate.

An awful tempest mashed the air,
The clouds were gaunt and few—
A black, as of a spectre's cloak,
Hid heaven and earth from view.

The creatures chuckled on the roofs
And whistled in the air,
And shook their fists and gnashed their teeth,
And swung their frenzied hair—

The morning lit, the birds arose—
The monster's faded eyes
Turned slowly to his native coast,
And peace was Paradise!

If I can stop one heart from breaking
I shall not live in vain,
If I can ease one life the aching
Or cool one pain,
Or help one fainting robin
Unto his nest again,
I shall not live in vain.

Forbidden fruit a flavor has
That lawful orchards mocks—
How luscious lies the pea within
The pod that duty locks!

A bird came down the walk—
He did not know I saw;
He bit an angleworm in halves
And ate the fellow, raw.

And then he drank a dew
From a convenient grass,
And then hopped sidewise to the wall
To let a beetle pass.

He glanced with rapid eyes
That hurried all abroad—
They looked like frightened beads, I thought—
He stirred his velvet head—

Like one in danger; cautious,
I offered him a crumb,
And he unrolled his feathers
And rowed him softer home

Than oars divide the ocean,
Too silver for a seam,
Or butterflies, off banks of noon,
Leap, plashless, as they swim.

Two butterflies went out at noon
And waltzed upon a farm,
Then stepped straight through the firmament
And rested on a beam

And then together bore away
Upon a shining sea,
Though never yet, in any port,
Their coming mentioned be.

If spoken by the distant bird,
If met in ether sea
By frigate, or by merchantman,
No notice was to me.

I never saw a moor,
I never saw the sea,
Yet know I how the heather looks,
And what a wave must be.

I never spoke with God,
Nor visited in heaven,
Yet certain am I of the spot
As if the chart were given.

You've seen balloons set, haven't you?
So stately they ascend
It is as swans discarded you
For duties diamond.

Their liquid feet go softly out
Upon a sea of blond,
They spurn the air as 'twere too mean
For creatures so renowned.

Their ribbons just beyond the eye,
They struggle some for breath,
And yet the crowd applauds below—
They would not encore death.

The gilded creature strains and spins,
Trips frantic in a tree,
Tears open her imperial veins
And tumbles in the sea.

The crowd retire with an oath
The dust in streets goes down,
And clerks in counting rooms observe,
'' 'Twas only a balloon.''

To make a prairie it takes a clover and one bee—
One clover, and a bee,
And revery.
The revery alone will do
If bees are few.

The pedigree of honey
Does not concern the bee—
A clover, any time, to him
Is aristocracy.

I'll tell you how the sun rose—
A ribbon at a time.
The steeples swam in amethyst,
The news like squirrels ran.

The hills untied their bonnets,
The bobolinks begun.
Then I said softly to myself,
"That must have been the sun!"

But how he set I know not.
There seemed a purple stile
Which little yellow boys and girls
Were climbing all the while

Till when they reached the other side,
A dominie in gray
Put gently up the evening bars,
And led the flock away.

My river runs to thee—
Blue sea, wilt welcome me?

My river waits reply.
Oh sea, look graciously!

I'll fetch thee brooks
From spotted nooks—

Say, sea,
Take me!

An everywhere of silver,
With ropes of sand
To keep it from effacing
The track called land.

I started early, took my dog,
And visited the sea—
The mermaids in the basement
Came out to look at me,

And frigates in the upper floor
Extended hempen hands,
Presuming me to be a mouse
Aground, upon the sands.

But no man moved me till the tide
Went past my simple shoe,
And past my apron and my belt,
And past my bodice too,

And made as he would eat me up
As wholly as a dew
Upon a dandelion's sleeve—
And then I started too—

And he—he followed close behind;
I felt his silver heel
Upon my ankle—then my shoes
Would overflow with pearl.

Until we met the solid town,
No one he seemed to know—
And bowing, with a mighty look
At me, the sea withdrew.

'Twas such a little, little boat
That toddled down the bay!
'Twas such a gallant, gallant sea
That beckoned it away!

'Twas such a greedy, greedy wave
That licked it from the coast—
Nor ever guessed the stately sails
My little craft was lost!

I hide myself within my flower,
That wearing on your breast,
You, unsuspecting, wear me too—
And angels know the rest.

I hide myself within my flower,
That fading from your vase,
You, unsuspecting, feel for me
Almost a loneliness.

A sepal, petal, and a thorn
Upon a common summer's morn,
A flash of dew, a bee or two,
A breeze,
A caper in the trees—

And I'm a rose!

Presentiment is that long shadow on the lawn
Indicative that suns go down;
The notice to the startled grass
That darkness is about to pass.

Will there really be a morning?
Is there such a thing as day?
Could I see it from the mountains
If I were as tall as they?

Has it feet like water lilies?
Has it feathers like a bird?
Is it brought from famous countries
Of which I have never heard?

Oh, some scholar! Oh, some sailor!
Oh, some wise man from the skies!
Please to tell a little pilgrim
Where the place called morning lies!

The moon was but a chin of gold
A night or two ago;
And now she turns her perfect face
Upon the world below.

Her forehead is of amplest blonde,
Her cheek like beryl stone,
Her eye unto the summer dew
The likest I have known.

Her lips of amber never part,
But what must be the smile
Upon her friend she could bestow,
Were such her silver will.

And what a privilege to be
But the remotest star,
For certainly her way might pass
Beside your twinkling door.

Her bonnet is the firmament,
The universe her shoe,
The stars the trinkets at her belt,
Her dimities of blue.

I know some lonely houses off the road
A robber'd like the look of—
Wooden-barred,
And windows hanging low,
Inviting to
A portico,
Where two could creep:
One hand the tools,
The other peep
To make sure all's asleep.
Old-fashioned eyes,
Not easy to surprise!

How orderly the kitchen'd look by night,
With just a clock—
But they could gag the tick,
And mice won't bark—
And so the walls don't tell,
None will.

A pair of spectacles ajar just stir—
An almanac's aware.
Was it the mat winked,
Or a nervous star?
The moon slides down the stair
To see who's there.

There's plunder—where?
Tankard, or spoon,
Earring, or stone,
A watch, some ancient brooch
To match the grandmamma,
Staid sleeping there.

Day rattles too,
Stealth's slow—
The sun has got as far
As the third sycamore.
Screams chanticleer,
"Who's there?"
And echoes, trains away,
Sneer—"Where?"
While the old couple, just astir,
Fancy the sunrise left the door ajar!

The grass so little has to do—
A sphere of simple green,
With only butterflies to brood,
And bees to entertain,

And stir all day to pretty tunes
The breezes fetch along,
And hold the sunshine in its lap
And bow to everything

And thread the dews, all night, like pearls,
And make itself so fine—
A duchess were too common
For such a noticing.

And even when it dies, to pass
In odors so divine,
As lowly spices gone to sleep,
Or amulets of pine.

And then to dwell in sovereign barns,
And dream the days away—
The grass so little has to do,
I wish I were the hay!

A narrow fellow in the grass
Occasionally rides;
You may have met him—did you not,
His notice sudden is.

The grass divides as with a comb,
A spotted shaft is seen;
And then it closes at your feet
And opens further on.

He likes a boggy acre,
A floor too cool for corn,
Yet when a child, and barefoot,
I more than once, at morn,

Have passed, I thought, a whiplash
Unbraiding in the sun—
When, stooping to secure it,
It wrinkled, and was gone.

Several of nature's people
I know, and they know me—
I feel for them a transport
Of cordiality;

But never met this fellow,
Attended or alone,
Without a tighter breathing,
And zero at the bone.

The bee is not afraid of me,
I know the butterfly.
The pretty people in the woods
Receive me cordially.

The brooks laugh louder when I come,
The breezes madder play.
Wherefore, mine eyes, thy silver mists?
Wherefore, O summer's day?

55

The show is not the show,
But they that go.
Menagerie to me
My neighbor be.
Fair play—
Both went to see.

Funny to be a century,
And see the people going by—
I should die of the oddity,
But then, I'm not so staid as he.

He keeps his secrets safely—very;
Were he to tell, extremely sorry
This bashful globe of ours would be—
So dainty of publicity.

The morns are meeker than they were,
The nuts are getting brown,
The berry's cheek is plumper,
The rose is out of town.

The maple wears a gayer scarf,
The field a scarlet gown.
Lest I should be old-fashioned,
I'll put a trinket on.

Apparently with no surprise
To any happy flower,
The frost beheads it at its play
In accidental power.
The blond assassin passes on,
The sun proceeds unmoved
To measure off another day
For an approving God.

I robbed the woods—
The trusting woods.
The unsuspecting trees
Brought out their burrs and mosses
My fantasy to please.
I scanned their trinkets curious—
I grasped—I bore away—
What will the solemn hemlock—
What will the oak tree say?

It sifts from leaden sieves,
It powders all the wood,
It fills with alabaster wool
The wrinkles of the road.

It makes an even face
Of mountain and of plain—
Unbroken forehead from the east
Unto the east again.

It reaches to the fence,
It wraps it, rail by rail,
Till it is lost in fleeces.
It flings a crystal veil

On stump and stack and stem—
The summer's empty room,
Acres of seams where harvests were,
Recordless, but for them.

It ruffles wrists of posts,
As ankles of a queen—
Then stills its artisans like ghosts,
Denying they have been.

The sky is low, the clouds are mean,
A traveling flake of snow
Across a barn or through a rut
Debates if it will go.

A narrow wind complains all day
How some one treated him—
Nature, like us, is sometimes caught
Without her diadem.

The judge is like the owl,
I've heard my father tell,
And owls do build in oaks—
So here's an amber sill

That slanted in my path
When going to the barn,
And if it serve you for a house,
Itself is not in vain—

About the price—'tis small—
I only ask a tune
At midnight. Let the owl select
His favorite refrain.

A word is dead
When it is said,
Some say.
I say it just
Begins to live
That day.

Make me a picture of the sun—
So I can hang it in my room
And make believe I'm getting warm
When others call it "Day"!

Draw me a robin on a stem—
So I am hearing him, I'll dream,
And when the orchards stop their tune,
Put my pretense away.

Say if it's really warm at noon,
Whether it's buttercups that "skim,"
Or butterflies that "bloom"?
Then skip the frost upon the lea,
And skip the russet on the tree,
Let's play those never come!

The wind tapped like a tired man,
And like a host, "Come in,"
I boldly answered; entered then
My residence within

A rapid, footless guest,
To offer whom a chair
Were as impossible as hand
A sofa to the air.

No bone had he to bind him,
His speech was like the push
Of numerous hummingbirds at once
From a superior bush.

His countenance a billow,
His fingers, if he pass,
Let go a music, as of tunes
Blown tremulous in glass.

He visited, still flitting;
Then, like a timid man,
Again he tapped—'twas flurriedly—
And I became alone.

Dear March, come in!
How glad I am!
I looked for you before.
Put down your hat—
You must have walked—
How out of breath you are!
Dear March, how are you?
And the rest?
Did you leave Nature well?
Oh, March, come right upstairs with me,
I have so much to tell!

I got your letter, and the birds'—
The maples never knew
That you were coming—I declare,
How red their faces grew!
But, March, forgive me—
And all those hills
You left for me to hue—
There was no purple suitable,
You took it all with you.

Who knocks? That April!
Lock the door!
I will not be pursued!
He stayed away a year, to call
When I am occupied.
But trifles look so trivial
As soon as you have come,
That blame is just as dear as praise
And praise as mere as blame.

Hope is the thing with feathers
That perches in the soul,
And sings the tune without the words,
And never stops at all.

And sweetest in the gale is heard—
And sore must be the storm
That could abash the little bird
That kept so many warm.

I've heard it in the chillest land,
And on the strangest sea—
Yet, never, in extremity,
It asked a crumb of me.

It's all I have to bring today,
This, and my heart beside,
This, and my heart, and all the fields,
And all the meadows wide.
Be sure you count, should I forget—
Some one the sum could tell—
This, and my heart, and all the bees
Which in the clover dwell.

Glossary

abash confuse, embarrass or ruffle. In "Hope is the thing with feathers," page 78, you can read the word to mean "stop the bird from singing."

affronts insults, abuses, causes to withdraw (like the turtle). See "Too much of proof affronts belief," page 7.

ajar Emily Dickinson's own dictionary (*Webster's Dictionary*, 1851) gives the meaning as "partly open, as a door." See "I know some lonely houses off the road," page 51.

alabaster a shining white, like the ground-up mineral called gypsum, from which shiny objects like lamp bases and small statues are made. So, in the poem "It sifts from leaden sieves," page 67, the snow falls like fine flour from lead-colored (gray) clouds, and piles up like shining white wool.

amber yellowish-brown, like the resin of that name and color. See "The judge is like the owl," page 69.

amethyst a violet or purplish color, like the gem of that name. See "I'll tell you how the sun rose," page 30.

amulets good-luck charms. In Emily's dictionary, "something worn as a remedy or preservative against evils or mischief." (Pine is a sweet-smelling wood.) See "The grass so little has to do," page 52.

aromatic sweet-smelling. See "Pink, small, and punctual," page 7.

artisans people skilled in making clever or useful things. We often call them craftspeople. See "It sifts from leaden sieves," page 67.

attended that is, when a friend was with her. See "A narrow fellow in the grass," page 54.

bailiff a person whose job is to keep order in a court of law. His "hymn" may be the sing-song list of instructions he must call out so that everyone will know what to do. See "A prompt, executive bird is the jay," page 13.

beryl stone a mineral of which beautiful gems are made, like emeralds (green) and aquamarine (blue). See "The moon was but a chin of gold," page 47.

Boanerges meaning a "fire-and-brimstone" kind of preacher. The name means "sons of thunder" and was given, according to the Bible, to James and John, who wanted to call down "fire from heaven" on the Samaritans (Luke ix. 54). See "I like to see it lap the miles," page 5.

bobolinks birds with a song that sounds to English-speaking listeners like "Bob o' Lincoln." In the spring, the males—normally brownish-yellow like the females—become black and white. They live in North and South America, as far south as Paraguay. See "I'll tell you how the sun rose," page 30.

bodice	the upper part of a dress, from the waist to the neck. When the tide went "past my bodice," it was already at the chin! See "I started early, took my dog," page 36.
candid	Emily's dictionary says, "fair, open, frank." See "Pink, small, and punctual," page 7.
chanticleer	a lovely French name for a rooster. It means "clear singer." See "I know some lonely houses off the road," page 51.
counting rooms	special rooms where business people keep their accounts. See "You've seen balloons set, haven't you?", page 27.
coursers	horses that can run swiftly. See "There is no frigate like a book," page 6.
covert	hidden or secret. See "Pink, small, and punctual," page 7.
diadem	a crown: perhaps the adornment of a shining sun for a smiling day—very different from the day described in "The sky is low, the clouds are mean," page 68.
diamond	Since diamond is a precious stone, the poet uses it as a descriptive word meaning precious or rare. See "You've seen balloons set, haven't you?", page 27.
dimities	gowns made of a material called dimity—very light, gauzy fabric woven with stripes in a heavier thread. In Emily's dictionary, "a kind of white cotton cloth, ribbed or figured." Perhaps the stripes are the clouds, or the last streaks of light in the dark-blue night sky. See "The moon was but a chin of gold," page 47.
docile	dutiful or obedient. Emily's dictionary says, "teachable . . . easily managed." See "I like to see it lap the miles," page 5.
dominie	a pastor or minister or (in the original Scottish meaning) schoolmaster, since each one has his flock. See "I'll tell you how the sun rose," page 31.
effacing	erasing, wiping out, or destroying. See "An everywhere of silver," page 34.
ether sea	the clear sky, which the ancient Greeks thought was filled with a substance called ether. See "Two butterflies went out at noon," page 23.
executive	someone in charge of getting work done quickly and well. See "A prompt, executive bird is the jay," page 13.
fantasy	fancy, whim, or imagination. In Emily's dictionary, "fantasy" and "fancy" are the same. See "I robbed the woods," page 65.
firmament	the open sky. See "Two butterflies went out at noon," page 23.
forswears	Nature denies her real age, and acts as young as she feels, all decked out with the little arbutus blossom. See "Pink, small, and punctual," page 7.
frigate	a fast naval vessel common in the eighteenth and early nineteenth centuries. See "There is no frigate like a book," page 6, "I started early, took my dog," page 36, and "Two butterflies went out at noon," page 23.

frugal	thrifty or economical. See "There is no frigate like a book," page 6.
hempen	made from a very tough fiber called hemp, out of which ropes are made—the ropes of the old sailing vessels in "I started early, took my dog," page 36.
inquest	a word used in law to mean looking into, or investigating, a crime. In "The mountain sat upon the plain," page 11, the mountain sees everything and looks into everything. He's a stern judge in the first stanza, a kindly grandfather in the second.
menagerie	a collection of wild animals, usually shown in zoos or circuses. See "The show is not the show," page 57.
merchantman	a ship used by merchants to carry their goods for trade. See "Two butterflies went out at noon," page 23.
mien	appearance, or bearing, or look. See "A prompt executive bird is the jay," page 13.
omnifold	a made-up word meaning "of everything"—that is, the mountain in "The mountain sat upon the plain," page 11, "sees everything."
omnipotent	all-powerful. See "I like to see it lap the miles," page 5.
pedigree	ancestry, especially the "right" kind of ancestry, as approved by stuffy people. See "The pedigree of honey," page 29.
plashless	without a splash. (A butterfly swimming in the air doesn't make any splash!) See "A bird came down the walk," page 22.
portico	a covered walk, its roof held up by columns. See "I know some lonely houses off the road," page 49.
presentiment	a feeling of something about to happen. Usually the feeling is only in the mind, but here the poet likens it to those lengthening shadows that warn you of sundown coming. See "Presentiment is that long shadow on the lawn," page 43.
pretense	make-believe. In "Make me a picture of the sun," page 73, the poet says that with a picture and a tune, she will pretend to be in the meadow with the robin and the sun— until evening comes. In the last stanza, she is saying that sorrow or sickness has kept her so long from the joy of outdoors that she can hardly remember what skims and what blooms. She and the artist must pretend that the end of the summer never comes!
prodigious	amazing in its power. See "I like to see it lap the miles," page 5.
refrain	song. See "The judge is like the owl," page 70.
revery	daydreaming. See "To make a prairie it takes a clover and one bee," page 28.
sepal	part of the "outer covering of a flower" (according to Emily's dictionary) or calyx. See "A sepal, petal, and a thorn," page 41.

shanties	small huts where the workmen who built the railroads lived. See "I like to see it lap the miles," page 5.
sill	the timber beneath a window or door. See "The judge is like the owl," page 69.
sovereign	kingly. See "The grass so little has to do," page 52.
spectre	ghost, goblin, the "monster" whose "cloak" blackens the sky in "An awful tempest mashed the air," page 15.
sphere	a space, or domain. See "The grass so little has to do," page 52.
staid	dignified. Emily's dictionary says, "sober; grave; steady; composed; regular." See "I know some lonely houses off the road," page 50, and "Funny to be a century," page 59.
stile	a set of steps or rungs to let people climb over a fence or wall without letting the cows through. See "I'll tell you how the sun rose," page 31.
supercilious	proud, haughty, or snobbish. (It comes from the Latin words meaning "raising an eyebrow.") In "I like to see it lap the miles," page 5, the train is proud of its power.
tankard	a large, ornamental drinking cup with a handle and a hinged cover. See "I know some lonely houses off the road," page 50.
toll	fee or charge. See "There is no frigate like a book," page 6.
track	a path or road. But perhaps Emily meant "tract"—that is, region or area. In the dictionary she used, one definition of "tract" is "track." We can make our own guess as to which she meant in "An everywhere of silver," page 34. Either one is fine!
transport	rapture, or ecstasy, or blissful joy. See "A narrow fellow in the grass," page 53.
traverse	journey, or crossing (of the ocean). See "There is no frigate like a book," page 6.
tremulous	shaking, or trembling, or perhaps—since "The wind tapped like a tired man," page 75, refers to tunes—vibrating.
warrant	a document issued by a magistrate, giving an officer the authority to make an arrest, conduct a search, seize someone's property, or act on other orders given by the court. See "A prompt, executive bird is the jay," page 13. Emily had great respect for those blue jays!

Designed by Barbara Holdridge

Composed in ITC Benguiat Book and Benguiat Medium by
Westcott Graphics, Baltimore, Maryland

Color separation by Capper, Inc., Knoxville, Tennessee

Printed on 80-pound Glatfelter Old Forge Opaque, smooth
finish, by Kingsport Press, Kingsport, Tennessee

Bound in paper and hardbound in Kivar 6 Homespun by
Kingsport Press, Kingsport, Tennessee